PERFORMANCE
EDITIONS

LABORUM
DULCE
LENIMEN

G. SCHIRMER

KUHLAU
SELECTED SONATINAS
Opus 20, Nos. 1-3, Opus 55, Nos. 1-3, Opus 88, No. 3

Edited and Recorded by Jennifer Linn

T0071556

To access companion recorded performances online, visit:
www.halleonard.com/mylibrary

Enter Code
3180-3882-1293-5348

On the cover:
The Fishery at Sletten

by Frederick Kjaerskod
(ca. 1836)

© Peter Harholdt/CORBIS

ISBN 978-1-4234-3114-5

G. SCHIRMER, Inc.

DISTRIBUTED BY
HAL•LEONARD®
CORPORATION
7777 W. BLUEMOUND RD. P.O. BOX 13819 MILWAUKEE, WI 53213

www.musicsalesclassical.com
www.halleonard.com

CONTENTS

The price of this publication includes access to companion recorded performances online, for download or streaming, using the unique code found on the title page.
Visit **www.halleonard.com/mylibrary** and enter the access code.

HISTORICAL NOTES

FRIEDRICH KUHLAU (1786-1832)

Friedrich Kuhlau was a German-born Danish composer who is best known as a composer of piano music. He was born in Uelzen, a small German town located between Hanover and Hamburg, on September 11, 1786. His father was an oboist, and a military bandsman by profession. At age seven, Kuhlau suffered an unfortunate accident, falling on a slippery street during the winter. As a result, he lost the use of his right eye for the remainder of his life. Kuhlau's earliest musical training is unknown, though it is likely his parents provided lessons as a youth. In 1800, after completing general schooling at the age of 14, Kuhlau moved to Hamburg, studying composition and theory with C.F.G. Schwenke, a highly respected local musician who was a former pupil of C.P.E. Bach. In 1806, Kuhlau had his first pieces published, a set of twelve variations and solos for flute, six waltzes for piano, and three songs for voice and piano.

Napoleon's France annexed Hamburg in 1810 and Kuhlau left the city in fear of being conscripted into the French army, in spite of his physical handicap. Kuhlau fled to Copenhagen, Denmark, under the guise of a concert tour. Once there, Kuhlau worked to establish himself as a composer and performer. He was appointed a court chamber musician in 1813, and his first opera, the singspiel Røverborgen, premiered in 1814 at the Royal Theatre, to critical and popular renown. His second opera, Trylleharpen, premiered in 1817, but met with significantly less acclaim. Kuhlau traveled to Vienna in 1821 and 1825, the latter trip resulting in a meeting with his musical hero, Beethoven. The two composers spent a boisterous evening of music-making and drinking together, with Beethoven composing a canon on Kuhlau's name ("Kühl, nicht lau," WoO 191) to commemorate the occasion. Kuhlau's greatest public success came for his incidental music to Elverhøj, a play written to honor the wedding of the King of Denmark's daughter in 1828. A piece Kuhlau composed for the play was later adopted as one of Denmark's two national anthems ("King Christian Stood by the Lofty Mast"). Shortly after the performance, Kuhlau was appointed honorary professor in the royal court.

While never without work, Kuhlau's appointments did not generate a significant income. As a result, he composed numerous pieces for flute to supplement his earnings, flute music being in high demand during his lifetime in Europe. While these pieces are highly idiomatic, Kuhlau was himself not a flutist, instead relying on a colleague in the royal orchestra for assistance in composing for the instrument. He also composed a significant amount of vocal music, including five operas, over 80 songs, a cantata, and several vocal canons. This music was composed with the latest European styles in mind, showing the influence of Cherubini, Weber, and Rossini.

Tragedy struck often for Kuhlau late in life. Both of his parents, with whom he was very close, died in 1830. On February 5, 1831, fire swept through his apartment building in Copenhagen, destroying all of his unpublished music. As a result of the fire, Kuhlau developed a chest illness that would eventually cost him his life. Kuhlau died in Copenhagen on March 12, 1832. He remains a renowned national music figure in Denmark, and his flute and piano music still enjoy popularity today.

—*Christopher Ruck*

PERFORMANCE NOTES

The Piano Sonatinas

Kuhlau is best known today as a composer of piano music. He began giving regular piano recitals in 1804 while in Hamburg, and wrote a piano concerto in 1810. His recital programs regularly included Beethoven, and Kuhlau's piano concerto and large-scale piano sonatas were often inspired by the German master. Kuhlau enjoyed significant success as a pianist on his tours to Scandanavia, where his recitals were highly acclaimed, particularly in Sweden. There is no clear evidence regarding Kuhlau's piano teaching; his highly accessible Sonatinas were written primarily to augment his income. However, these pieces address significant pedagogical issues, scales and arpeggios in particular, that prepare pianists for the demands of Beethoven's piano music and show a deep understanding of the instrument. They remain staples of most intermediate level pianists. The three sonatinas of Op. 20 were first published in 1819; the six sonatinas of Op. 55 were first published in 1823 in Copenhagen. The four pieces of Op. 88 were published in Copenhagen in 1827.

Sonatina Levels

While Clementi's Op. 36 Sonatinas were conceived with a clear pedagogical and progressive order in mind, Kuhlau's sonatinas vary in difficulty within each opus and even movement to movement within each sonatina. This requires more forethought in assigning pieces from this collection in a progressive order. I have included a chart with suggested pedagogical elements and leveling as a guide for making selections to fit a particular student's needs.

Beethoven's Broadwood grand piano 1818

Leveling Chart

Page	Sonatina	Tempo	Key	Meter	Rhythm elements	Challenge elements	Length (pages)	Length (measures)	Level
	Op. 20, No. 1								
10		Allegro	C	4/4		Alberti bass/tempo control	4	80	7
14		Andante	F	6/8		Phrase shaping & balance	1	16	7
15		Rondo: Allegro	C	2/4		Fast Alberti bass	6	157	8
	Op. 20, No. 2								
21		Allegro	G	3/4		Tempo & articulation control	5	158	9
26		Adagio e sostenuto	E♭	2/4		Pedal technique, trills, balance	2	49	9
28		Allegro scherzando	G	6/8		Fast scales & leaps	6	130	9
	Op. 20, No. 3								
34		Allegro	F	4/4		Tempo control, grace notes	6	114	8
40		Larghetto	B♭	6/8		Articulation & balance	3	46	8
43		Alla Polacca	F	3/4		Fast continuous scales	7	116	9
	Op. 55, No. 1								
51		Allegro	C	4/4		Alberti bass	3	62	6
54		Vivace	C	3/8		Chromatic scales	4	116	6
	Op. 55, No. 2								
59		Allegretto	G	3/4		Ties and turns	3	52	6
62		Cantabile	C	3/4		Balance, parallel sixths	2	20	6
64		Allegro	G	2/4		Chromatic scales, jumps, Alberti bass	7	129	7
	Op. 55, No. 3								
72		Allegro con spirito	C	4/4		Right & left hand scales	4	58	7
76		Allegretto grazioso	C	2/4		Articulation, contrasting touches	6	122	7
	Op. 88, No. 3								
82		Allegro con affetto	Am	4/4		Tempo control, RH scales	4	62	6
86		Andantino	F	6/8		LH finger pedaling	2	27	6
88		Allegro burlesco	Am	2/4		Chromatic scales, acciacaturas	6	120	8

Sonatinas: Valuable and Enjoyable

The inherent value of sonatina study for the developing pianist has kept this genre of pieces in the forefront of intermediate piano literature for generations. Students who play a healthy number of sonatinas may start out as somewhat awkward beginners, but blossom into agile and stylistic pianists within just a few short years of studying these pedagogical gems. The metamorphosis is exciting and provides great motivation to the student and teacher.

Students love playing sonatinas because they are introduced to new musical and physical challenges in a way that does not overwhelm their developing technique or stylistic understanding. They are able to create authentic-sounding music full of style and flair, but not without learning some essential new practice techniques along the way. The skills gained and the confidence built by playing the delightful sonatinas of Friedrich Kuhlau make them the perfect repertoire staple for intermediate piano students of any age.

Preparation of the Edition

In this edition of selected Sonatinas by Friedrich Kuhlau, the first published editions were researched and used as the basis for notation and articulation, made available courtesy of the Sibley Music Library, Kuhlau Collection, Eastman School of Music. These editions include the Breitkopf & Härtel edition and the C.C. Lose edition of the Opus 20 Sonatinas (1820); Richter, Bechmann et Milde edition of the Opus 55 Sonatinas (1823), and the C.C. Lose edition of the Op. 88 Sonatinas (1827). Special thanks to Mr. David Peter Coppen, Special Collections Librarian and Archivist at the Sibley Music Library, Eastman School of Music.

Editorial additions or modifications to the articulations and dynamics in these first published editions are indicated with a bracket in the score. Fingerings and metronome markings have been included as suggestions by the editor. As an additional guide to the student, the editorial aspects of this edition correspond to the recorded performance, allowing the student to listen to an obtainable performance model.

Historical Perspective: Early Romanticism

Kuhlau's contribution to the sonatina repertoire came approximately a quarter century after Muzio Clementi composed the *Six Progressive Sonatinas, Op. 36* in 1797, and yet the tendency is to lump all sonatinas into one pedagogical and stylistic bin. Kuhlau's Op. 20 Sonatinas were composed in 1820, the same year that Chopin composed his first Mazurka at age ten. Kuhlau's Op. 55 and Op. 88 Sonatinas, Beethoven's late Piano Sonatas (Op. 109, 110, 111) and Schubert's *Moments Musicaux* were all composed in the mid 1820s, placing Kuhlau squarely in the transitional category of Early Romanticism. Although classical elements remain (i.e. Alberti bass, sonata-allegro form), there is an expressive, lyrical and romantic quality to Kuhlau's sonatinas that distinguish them from Clementi's earlier works.

Kuhlau: "Beethoven of the Flute"

Perhaps the lyricism in Kuhlau's music can be attributed in part to the flute. Kuhlau has become known as the "Beethoven of the flute" because of his extensive contributions to the flute repertoire. Although Kuhlau himself was not an accomplished flutist, his father taught flute and oboe in their home and Kuhlau did play the flute for a brief time as a child. The flute was an important compositional and as a result, financial vehicle for the composer, with nearly a quarter of his total works written for the instrument.

The flute's lyrical influence can be felt throughout his sonatinas from the acciaccaturas and challenging scale passages in fast movements,

Sonatina in A Minor, Op. 88, No. 3,
third movement, mm. 1-3

to the vocalise qualities of the slow movements, requiring the pianist to "breathe" to communicate the musical inflection suggested by the rests.

Sonatina in G Major, Op. 20, No. 2,
second movement, mm. 1-4

Articulation

In Muzio Clementi's *Introduction to the Art of Playing on the Piano Forte* [1801] he describes the various touches and articulations with great clarity:

SLUR

"called LEGATO in Italian, must be played in a SMOOTH and CLOSE manner"

In the Kuhlau Sonatinas there are many scale passages that do not have specific slurs indicated in the first editions. As to questions therefore about the desired touch, the logical conclusion can be found in Clementi's instruction: "When the composer leaves the LEGATO, and STACCATO to the performer's taste; the best rule is, to adhere chiefly to the LEGATO; reserving the STACCATO to give SPIRIT occasionally to certain passages and to set off the HIGHER BEAUTIES of the LEGATO."

The various staccato touches as described by Clementi are also employed throughout Kuhlau's Sonatinas:

STACCATO
Wedge:

"called in ITALIAN, STACCATO; denoting DISTINCTNESS, and SHORTNESS of sound; which is produced by lifting the finger up, as soon as it has struck the key"

Dot: "or they are marked thus

which, when composers are EXACT in their writing, means LESS staccato than the preceding mark (wedge); the finger, therefore, is kept down somewhat longer"

Portato: "or thus"

which means STILL LESS staccato: the nice degrees of MORE and LESS, however, depend on the CHARACTER, and PASSION of the piece; the STYLE of which must be WELL OBSERVED by the performer"

Pedaling

When making any decision about the use of the damper pedal in these sonatinas, we should remember their educational nature and the ability of the performer or student to achieve the necessary nuances. Although there were advances to the damper pedal mechanism during Kuhlau's life, it was still used primarily in slow movements, in broken-chord passages, or to warm the tone at cadence points. Sometimes the use of "finger pedaling" is notated by Kuhlau to sustain the harmony, especially when fast scale passages do not allow for the dampers to be raised without unstylistic blur.

Sonatina in C Major, Op. 20, No. 1,
third movement, mm. 60-63

Kuhlau also skillfully indicates this "finger pedaling" in slow passages which require a sustained harmony but require little or no use of the damper pedal.

Sonatina in A Minor, Op. 88, No. 3,
second movement, mm. 21-22

In movements marked with a *sostenuto*, it is clearly appropriate to use the damper pedal, being careful not to pedal through rests, allowing the music to "breathe."

Sonatina in F Major, Op. 20, No. 3,
second movement, mm. 1-2

Ornamentation

By the time Kuhlau's Sonatinas Op. 20, 55, and 88 were composed (1820-1827), the clear instructions for ornamentation written by Clementi in his *Introduction to the Art of Playing on the Piano Forte* (1801) were more than 20 years old and not strictly followed. Instead of listing Clementi's instructions for ornamentation, I chose instead to include individual realizations of appoggiaturas, turns, trills, and slides above selected ornaments in the score, providing suggestions in line with Classical era performance practice.

Dynamics

It is interesting to note that in the first published editions of Kuhlau's Sonatinas, numerous dynamic markings were, for the most part, clearly indicated. Any editorial changes or additions to the dynamics of the first edition(s) are shown in brackets.

The dynamic markings included in the first edition of the Clementi Sonatinas Op. 36 (1797) were sparse in comparison to the first editions of Kuhlau, suggesting a continuing improvement in the technology of music printing by the mid 1820s.

The pianoforte was also undergoing many improvements, and although its *forte* volume was still less than today's powerful concert grand, it was rapidly approaching the dynamic range of our modern instrument. With this in mind, the performer might wish to temper their fullest *fortissimo* down slightly, to achieve a more historically sound perspective.

—*Jennifer Linn*

Sonatina in C Major

I

Friedrich Kuhlau
Op. 20, No. 1

II

III

RONDO

Allegro [♩ = ca. 120]

Sonatina in G Major
I

Friedrich Kuhlau
Op. 20, No. 2

* The 1893 Schirmer edition and many other subsequent editions print  in this measure.

II

Adagio e sostenuto [♪ = ca. 66]

III

Sonatina in F Major

I

Friedrich Kuhlau
Op. 20, No. 3

* In the 1826 Breitkopf & Härtel edition this note is a B♭.

II

III

44

Sonatina in C Major

I

Friedrich Kuhlau
Op. 55, No. 1

II

Sonatina in G Major
I

Friedrich Kuhlau
Op. 55, No. 2

Allegretto [♩ = ca. 116]

II

Cantabile [♩ = ca. 69]

[*p*] *legato assai*

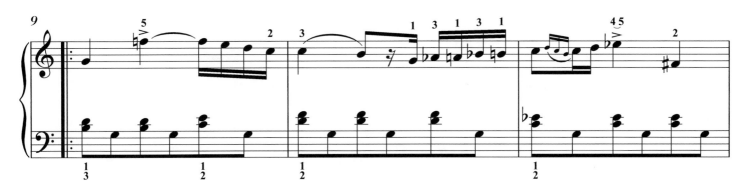

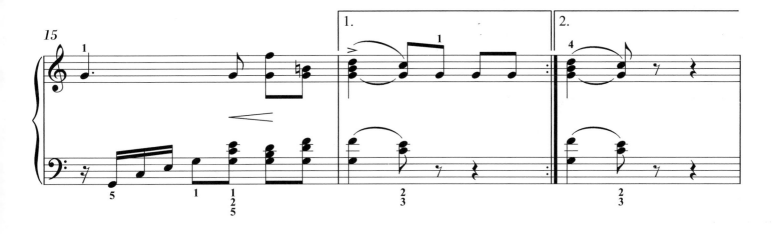

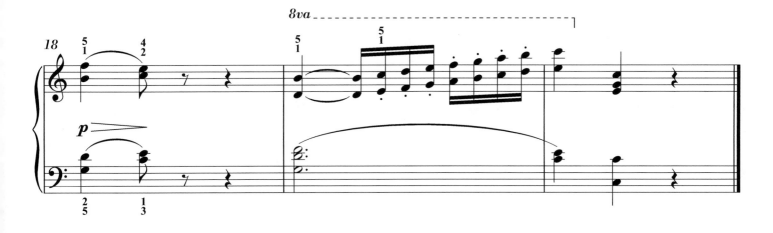

III

Allegro [♩ = ca. 104]

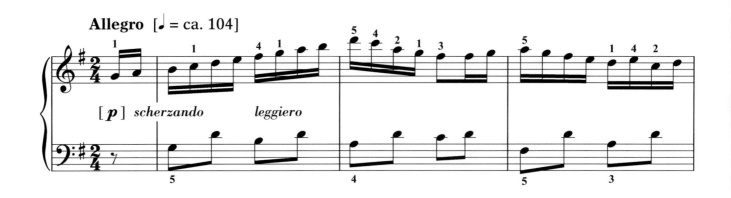

[**p**] *scherzando*   *leggiero*

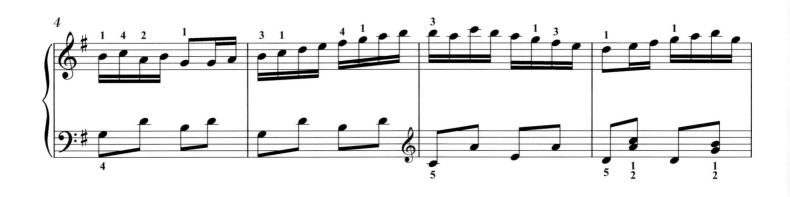

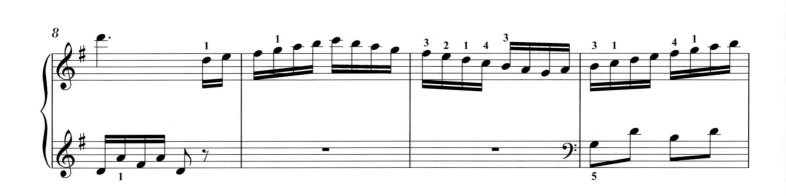

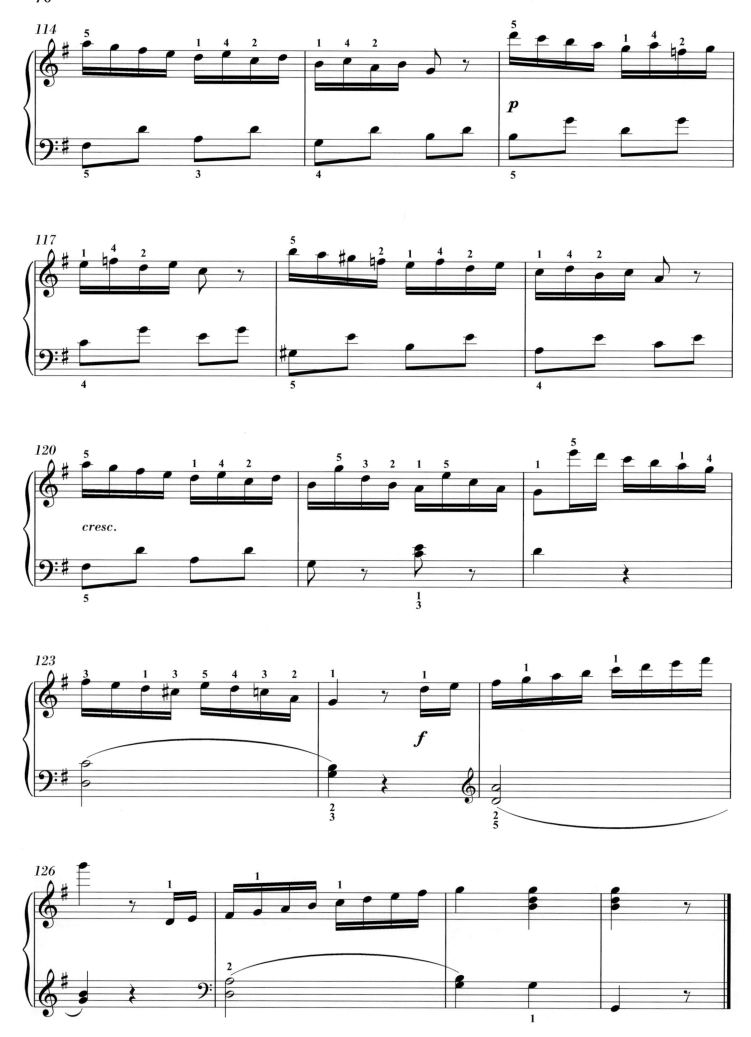

Sonatina in C Major

I

Friedrich Kuhlau
Op. 55, No. 3

Allegro con spirito [♩ = ca. 126]

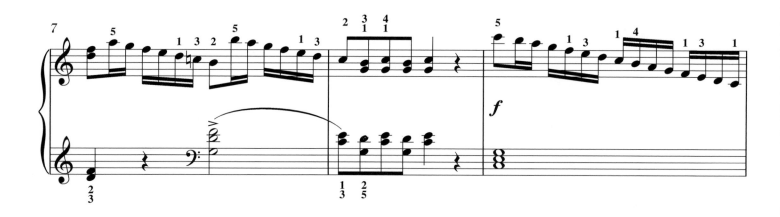

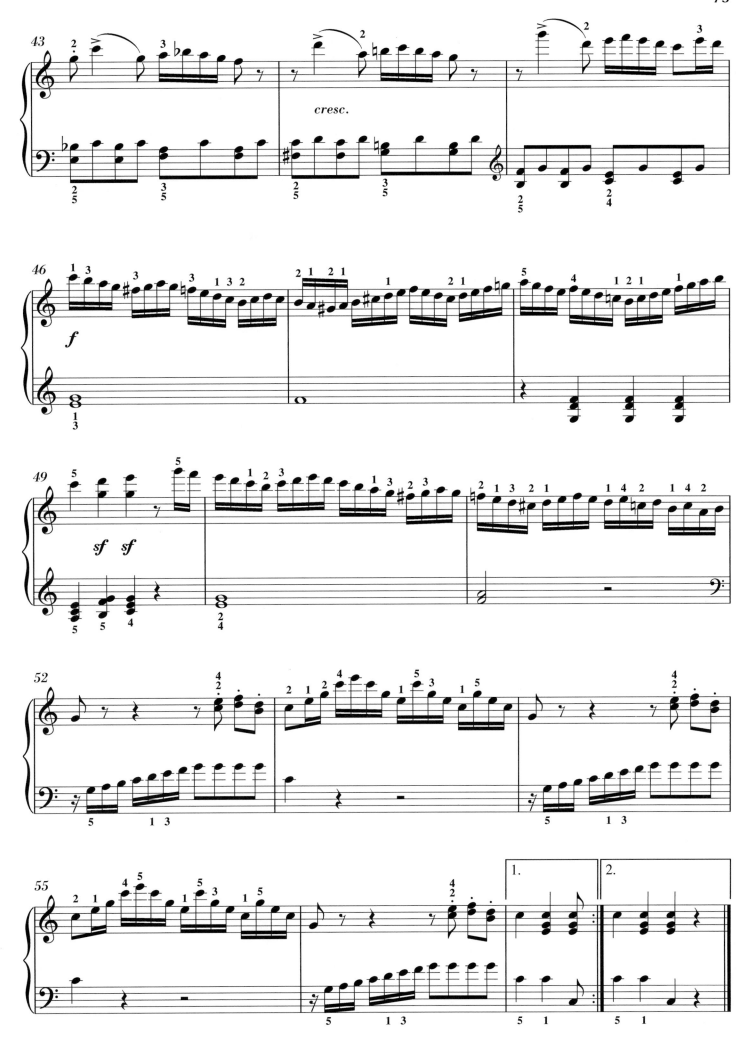

II

Allegretto grazioso [♩ = ca. 104]

Sonatina in A Minor

I

Friedrich Kuhlau
Op. 88, No. 3

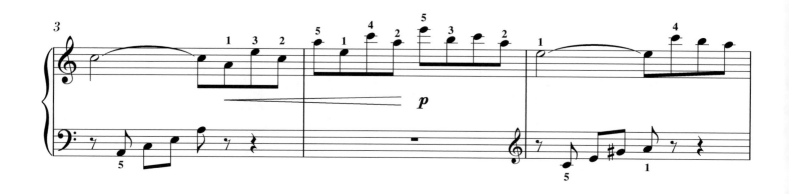

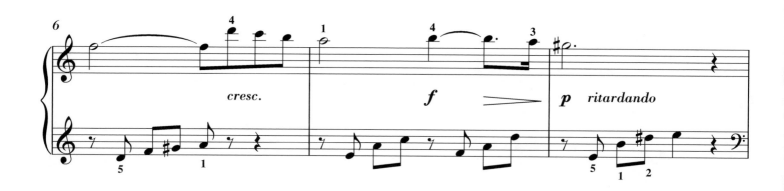

II

Andantino [♪ = ca. 132]

III

Allegro burlesco [♩ = ca. 132]

ABOUT THE EDITOR

JENNIFER LINN

An accomplished pianist, teacher, and clinician, Jennifer Linn holds the title of Creative Manager-Educational Piano for Hal Leonard Corporation. In addition to her contribution as a composer and arranger for the *Hal Leonard Student Piano Library*, her work includes serving as Editor and recording artist for the G. Schirmer Performance Editions *Clementi Sonatinas Op. 36*, *Kuhlau Selected Sonatinas*, and *Schumann Selections from Album for the Young, Op. 68*. Ms. Linn also served as Assistant Editor for the HLSPL Technique Classics *Hanon for the Developing Pianist* and *Czerny: Selections from the the Little Pianist, Opus 823*.

As a clinician, she has presented recitals, workshops, master classes and HLSPL showcases throughout the United States and Canada, including the World Piano Pedagogy Conference, Music Teachers National Association conventions, Music Teachers Association of California and MTNA state programs throughout the country. Many of her compositions have been selected for the National Federation of Music Clubs festival list and the London College of Music repertoire list and are frequently recommended in reviews by *Clavier* and *American Music Teacher* magazines.

Ms. Linn's teaching career spans more than 25 years and includes independent studio teaching of all ages, as well as group instruction and piano pedagogy at the university level. In 1999-2000, Ms. Linn served as visiting lecturer in piano pedagogy at the University of Illinois at Urbana-Champaign and has been on the faculty of the Illinois Summer Youth Music Piano Camp for several years. Her students have successfully competed in state and national level auditions. As an active member of MTNA, she has served as the composition chair for the West Central Division as well as vice president of the St. Louis Area Music Teachers Association. Ms. Linn received her B.M. with distinction and M.M. in piano performance from the University of Missouri-Kansas City Conservatory of Music where she was the winner of the concerto-aria competition. She was also named the outstanding student in the graduate piano division and given the prestigious vice chancellor's award for academic excellence and service.